KT-504-340

Poems chosen by
Richard Brown and Kate Ruttle

Illustrated by Martin Chatterton

CAMBRIDGE
UNIVERSITY PRESS

04249
04249

Cambridge Reading

General Editors
Richard Brown and Kate Ruttle

Consultant Editor
Jean Glasberg

Published by the Press Syndicate of the University of Cambridge
The Pitt Building, Trumpington Street, Cambridge CB2 1RP
40 West 20th Street, New York, NY10011-4211, USA
10 Stamford Road, Oakleigh, Melbourne 3166, Australia

First published 1996

Nonsense!
This selection © Richard Brown and Kate Ruttle 1996
Illustrations © Martin Chatterton 1996

Printed in Great Britain at the University Press, Cambridge

A catalogue record for this book is available from the British Library

ISBN 0 521 49995 X paperback

Acknowledgements

We are grateful to the following for permission to reproduce poems:
'"Quack!" Said the Billy-Goat' by Charles Causley from *Figgie Hobbin.* Macmillan.
'My Name Is . . .' by Pauline Clarke from *Roger was a Razor Fish*: edited by Jill
    Bennett. The Bodley Head.
'Fish Fingers' and 'Horrible Happenings' from *Songs for My Dog and Other People* by
    Max Fatchen. Copyright © Max Fatchen, 1980. First published by Viking Kestrel.
'The Apple and the Worm' by Robert Heidbreder from *Don't Eat Spiders.* Oxford
    University Press, Canada. Reproduced by permission of Stoddart Publishing Co. Ltd,
    Don Mills, Ontario, Canada.
'On the Ning Nang Nong' and 'A Little Worm' by Spike Milligan. Reproduced by
    permission of Spike Milligan Productions Ltd.
'Humpty Dumpty Went to the Moon' by Michael Rosen from *A Very First Poetry Book*.
    Oxford University Press.
'Tiger's Tea' © Claire Pulley, 1996.

Every effort has been made to reach copyright holders; the publishers would like to
hear from anyone whose rights they have unknowingly infringed.

Contents

On the Ning Nang Nong

On the Ning Nang Nong
Where the Cows go Bong!
And the Monkeys all say Boo!
There's a Nong Nang Ning
Where the trees go Ping!
And the tea pots Jibber Jabber Joo.
On the Nong Ning Nang
All the mice go Clang!
And you just can't catch 'em when they do!

So it's Ning Nang Nong!
Cows go Bong!
Nong Nang Ning!
Trees go Ping!
Nong Ning Nang!
The mice go Clang!
What a noisy place to belong,
Is the Ning Nang Ning Nang Nong!!

Spike Milligan

Fuzzy Wuzzy

Fuzzy Wuzzy was a bear
But Fuzzy Wuzzy had no hair,
So Fuzzy Wuzzy
Wasn't fuzzy, was he?

Anon

Algy and the Bear

Algy met a bear,
The bear met Algy.
The bear was bulgy . . .
The bulge was Algy.

Anon

Tiger's Tea

I kept a furry tiger to scare the thieves away.
I trained her to eat people; she ate one every day.

Now she's feeling hungry and it's nearly time
  for tea;
I have a funny feeling that she's got her eye on me.

Claire Pulley

The Crocodile

How doth the little crocodile
Improve his shining tail,
And pour the waters of the Nile
On every golden scale.

How cheerfully he seems
  to grin,
How neatly spreads his claws,
And welcomes little fishes in,
With gently smiling jaws.

Lewis Carroll

A Little Worm

Today I saw a little worm
Wriggling on his belly.
Perhaps he'd like to come inside
And see what's on the Telly.

Spike Milligan

The Apple and the Worm

I bit an apple
  That had a worm.
I swallowed the apple,
  I swallowed the worm.
I felt it squiggle,
  I felt it squirm.
I felt it wiggle,
  I felt it turn.
I felt it so slippery,
  Slimy, scummy,
I felt it land – PLOP –
  In my tummy!

I guess that worm is
  there to stay
Unless . . .
I swallow a bird some day!

Robert Heidbreder

"Quack!" Said the Billy-Goat

"Quack!" said the billy-goat.
"Oink!" said the hen.
"Miaow!" said the little chick
Running in the pen.

"Hobble-gobble!" said the dog.
"Cluck!" said the sow.
"Tu-whit tu-whoo!" the donkey said.
"Baa!" said the cow.

"Hee-haw!" the turkey cried.
The duck began to moo.
All at once the sheep went,
"Cock-a-doodle-doo!"

The owl coughed
And cleared his throat
And he began to bleat.
"Bow-wow!" said the cock
Swimming in the leat.

"Cheep-cheep!" said the cat
As she began to fly.
"Farmer's been and laid an egg –
That's the reason why."

Charles Causley

Old Hank

For a lark,
For a prank,
Old Hank
Walked a plank.
These bubbles mark

     0
         0
  0
       0
   0

Where Hank sank.

Anon

14

Horrible Happenings

When Aunt Louisa lit the gas
   She had the queerest feeling.
Instead of leaving by the door
   She vanished through the ceiling.

Max Fatchen

Fish Fingers

A fish had remarked to a chip,
"Unless we can give them the slip,
  When the fat starts to fry
  I'm afraid it's goodbye
And it won't be a very nice trip."

Max Fatchen

My Name Is . . .

My name is Sluggery-wuggery
My name is Worms-for-tea
My name is Swallow-the-table-leg
My name is Drink-the-Sea.

My name is I-eat-saucepans
My name is I-like-snails
My name is Grand-piano-George
My name is I-ride-whales.

My name is Jump-the-chimney
My name is Bite-my-knee
My name is Jiggery-pokery
And Riddle-me-ree, and ME.

Pauline Clarke

Peas

I always eat peas with honey,
I've done it all my life.
They do taste kind of funny
But it keeps them on the knife.

Anon

Humpty Dumpty Went to the Moon

Humpty Dumpty went to the moon
on a supersonic spoon.
He took some porridge and a tent
but when he landed
the spoon got bent.
Humpty said he didn't care
and for all I know
he's still up there.

Michael Rosen

Little Miss Muffet

Little Miss Muffet
Sat on a tuffet
Eating her Irish stew.
Along came a spider
Who sat down beside her
And so she ate him up too.

Anon

Little Miss Tucket

Little Miss Tucket
Sat on a bucket
Eating some peaches and cream.
There came a big spider
Who sat down beside her.
She said, "Go away or I'll scream!"

Anon

The Man Who Wasn't There

As I was going up the stair
I met a man who wasn't there.
He wasn't there again today –
Oh, how I wish he'd go away.

Anon

22

As I Was Going Out One Day

As I was going out one day
My head fell off and rolled away
But when I saw that it was gone
I picked it up and put it on.

And when I got into the street
A fellow cried, "Look at your feet!"
I looked at them and sadly said,
"I left them both asleep in bed."

Anon

Index of first lines